MW01293440

# Growing In The Garden

Dianne Bassett-Giehtbrock

Illustrated By: Jennifer Powell

*AuthorHouse™*
*1663 Liberty Drive*
*Bloomington, IN 47403*
*www.authorhouse.com*
*Phone: 1 (800) 839-8640*

© *2015 Dianne Bassett-Giehtbrock. All rights reserved.*
*Illustrated by: Jennifer Powell*

*No part of this book may be reproduced, stored in a retrieval system,*
*or transmitted by any means without the written permission of the author.*

*Published by AuthorHouse: 02/01/2016*

*ISBN: 978-1-5049-6798-3 (sc)*
*ISBN: 978-1-5049-6799-0 (e)*

*Library of Congress Control Number: 2015920791*

*Print information available on the last page.*

*Any people depicted in stock imagery provided by Thinkstock are models,*
*and such images are being used for illustrative purposes only.*
*Certain stock imagery* © *Thinkstock.*

*This book is printed on acid-free paper.*

*Because of the dynamic nature of the Internet, any web addresses or links contained in this book may have changed*
*since publication and may no longer be valid. The views expressed in this work are solely those of the author and do not*
*necessarily reflect the views of the publisher, and the publisher hereby disclaims any responsibility for them.*

author**HOUSE**°

To my husband and best friend, this book is dedicated to you. I am humbled by you daily. I am honored to spend every day together growing this beautiful life we share. It is no doubt that you learned to be a father from one of the best. May his memory continue to give you peace as you grow in your garden. To my buddy Ava, thank you for your continuous friendship and editing skills. Carrie Terrasi Grube, I am humbled by your knowledge of grammar and appreciate your help fine tuning my story. To my parents and brother Steve, I cherish my childhood memories and am lucky to learn about life with you close by. To my girls Paige and Chloe, it has been an amazing journey being your mom and you will always come first in my busy world. I can't wait to learn more about life through your eyes. I love you both with all I have.

2

"When you're planning out a garden,
there's a lot you need to know.
Mixing water, seeds, and dirt,
and sun will make things grow."

"Will you teach us, Daddy?"
Both girls run ahead.
"Let's start by dumping all our seeds
into the garden bed."

"Wait!" said Daddy.
"First, we'll dig some little rows
to hold the tiny seed.
Cover gently, not too deep,
and pull out all the weeds.

Sprinkle them with water,
so they don't get too dry.
Hope that Mother Nature
will send showers from the sky."

BOOM! A clap of thunder,
the rain comes pouring down.
Our thirsty garden soaks it up;
the dirt turns muddy brown.

Happy earthworms tunnel air
as they wiggle out.
It will help the seeds to breathe
as they begin to sprout.

"Daddy, look!  A rainbow!"
both girls shout together.
It's fun to be out gardening
in any kind of weather.

Mom arrives with lemonade
and cookies on a tray.
"You still have lots of work to do
before you end your day."

"Our next step is to build a fence,"
Daddy tells the girls.
"Most critters love to nibble
on carrot tops with curls.
We'll use wood and wire mesh
because it works the best."

Daddy hammers all the nails;
the girls help with the rest.

"We need to give our garden space
and wait for it to grow.
We also need to watch out
for the bugs that live below.

They will feast on our new plants
unless we use a spray.
Soapy water, lightly sprayed,
will shoo the beasts away."

14

"If we keep up with the watering
and weeding for a while,
our vegetables will grow,
and our flowers will show their style.

Finally at harvest time,
we'll pick and pluck and pull.
It's dirty work and messy,
but our buckets will be full."

16

"What happens in the winter?
Does the garden go to sleep?"
The girls sit next to Daddy,
and the crickets sing, "cheep cheep!"

"Yes, while you're out ice skating
or sliding down the snow,
the garden takes a quiet nap
like bunnies in their burrow."

18

"Then everything wakes up in Spring
like after a long night?
The critters all come back again?
Daddy, is that right?"

"Yes, squirrels will chase and bunnies race
through our garden rows.
We'll need to furrow fresh ones
then plant new seeds to grow."

20

"Gardens contain big super powers,
so share this secret with friends.
To create a garden with family,
the memories will never end."

# About the Author

Dianne Bassett Giehtbrock has a lifelong love of the outdoors, animals, and education. She teaches Kindergarten for the Holly Area School District. She grew up in Novi, Michigan where she earned a B.S. and M.A. degree in Education from Central Michigan University. Dianne taught Kindergarten in Palm Beach County, Florida for four years before moving back to Michigan where she taught in both the Novi and Clarkston Community School districts. Dianne loves to write children's books about her family, "I love to write about the simple joys in my life." Dianne's favorite vegetables to eat are green beans, and they are even better when she can grow them in her very own garden.

# About the Illustrator

**Jennifer Powell** has a lifelong love of art, education and the outdoors. Jennifer has a BA in education from Michigan State University and an MA from Eastern Michigan University. She has written and illustrated several children's books.  Jennifer lives in Mackinac County, Michigan with her husband and two sons. Her favorite vegetable to grow in the garden? Green beans.

CPSIA information can be obtained
at www.ICGtesting.com
Printed in the USA
LVOW05s1930220216
476256LV00016B/68/P